The Joy of Piano Duets

For centuries duet playing has held and continues to hold
a fascinating attraction for the student, the teacher,
the professional musician. One of the most pleasurable aspects
of music-making, it always provides an enjoyable experience
to both player and audience. In addition, it has definite
pedagogical benefits.

The Joy Of Piano Duets contains colorful examples of music
from the classics to folk songs and jazz. The arrangements
are equally easy for both players with the melody alternating
between the two.

Robert Schumann advised pianists, "Don't omit any opportunity
to play with others." It is sound advice. We trust that this
collection will be a source of pleasure to "one piano-four hands"
enthusiasts the world over.

Exclusive Distributors:
Hal Leonard 7777 West Bluemound Road, Milwaukee, WI 53213 Email: info@halleonard.com
Hal Leonard Europe Limited 42 Wigmore Street Marylebone, London, WIU 2 RY Email: info@halleonardeurope.com
Hal Leonard Australia Pty. Ltd. 4 Lentara Court Cheltenham, Victoria, 9132 Australia Email: info@halleonard.com.au

Piano recorded by Paul Knight.
CD mixed and mastered by Jonas Persson.

Printed in the EU.

Contents

Adeste Fideles .... Old Latin Hymn 78   CD track 33

Adios Muchachos .... Julio Sanders 68   CD track 29

Arioso .... Johann Sebastian Bach 10   CD track 4

Arkansas Traveler .... Fiddle Tune 64   CD track 27

Banjo Rag, The .... Charles Drumheller 60   CD track 25

Boogie For Two .... Gerald Martin 70   CD track 30

Bourrée *from*
      Violin Sonata No. 2 .... Johann Sebastian Bach 4   CD track 1

Can-Can *from the operetta*
      La Vie Parisienne .... Jacques Offenbach 54   CD track 23

Caprice No. 24 .... Niccolo Paganini 14   CD track 6

Careless Love .... Folk Song 62   CD track 26

Comedians' Galop, The .... Dmitri Kabalevsky 36   CD track 17

Duet *from Don Giovanni*
      "La ci darem la mano" ...... Wolfgang Amadeus Mozart 16   CD track 7

Fascination .... Filippo D. Marchetti 52   CD track 22

Frolic .... Béla Bartók 26   CD track 12

Gavotte *from*
      The Classical Symphony .... Serge Prokofieff 20   CD track 9

Give My Regards To Broadway .... George M. Cohan 74   CD track 31

Harmonious Blacksmith, The
      Theme .... Georg Friedrich Händel 24   CD track 11

Hush-A-Bye
      All The Pretty Little Horses .... Folk Lullaby 66   CD track 28

Jamaica Farewell .... Calypso Song 76   CD track 32

Little Rhapsody on *Hungarian themes* .... Denes Agay 38   CD track 18

Lullaby from *The Firebird* .... Igor Stravinsky 28   CD truck 13

Melody In Waltz Time *theme from*
      String Quartet No. 2 .... Alexander Borodin 18   CD track 8

Merry Boys Polka, The .... Franz von Suppé 42   CD track 19

Minuet *from*
      A Little Night Music .... Wolfgang Amadeus Mozart 32   CD track 15

Musical Snuffbox, The .... Anatol Liadov 22   CD track 10

O Come All Ye Faithful .... Old Latin Hymn 78   CD track 33

Parade Of The Tin Soldiers .... Leon Jessel 56   CD track 24

Rondino *theme from*
      Cello Concerto in D .... Joseph Haydn 12   CD track 5

Streets Of Laredo, The .... Cowboy Song 34   CD track 16

The Metronome *theme from*
      Symphony No.8 .... Ludwig van Beethoven 8   CD track 3

The Trout .... Franz Schubert 6   CD track 2

Trepak *Russian Dance from*
      The Nutcracker .... Peter I. Tchaikovsky 30   CD track 14

Waltzes *from Fledermaus*
      and *Gypsy Baron* .... Johann Strauss 44   CD track 20

Washington Post, The .... John Philip Sousa 48   CD track 21

Bourrée
from Violin Sonata No. 2

Secondo

Johann Sebastian Bach

L/R split 1

Lively

A

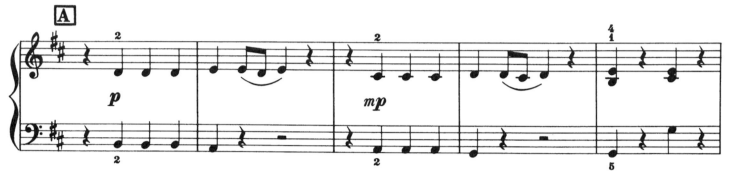

B

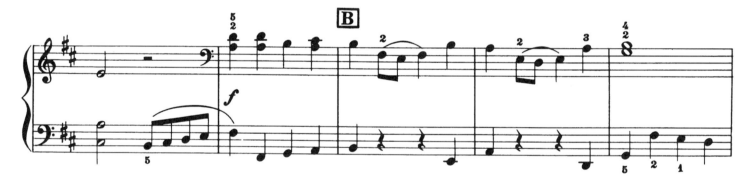

C

Bourrée
from Violin Sonata No. 2

Primo

Johann Sebastian Bach

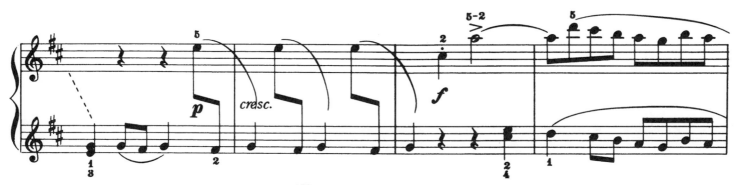

The Trout

Moderately   **Secondo**

Franz Schubert

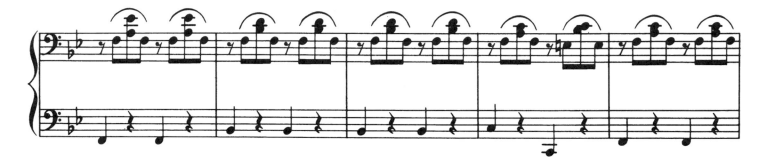

The Trout

Primo

Franz Schubert

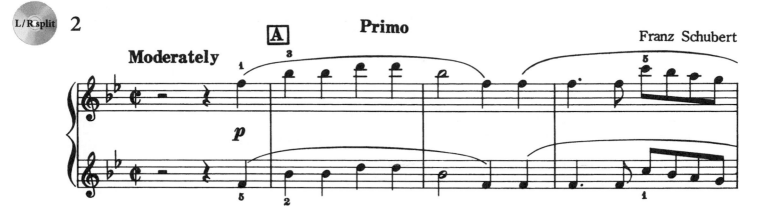

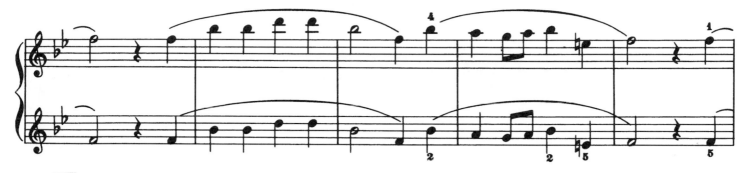

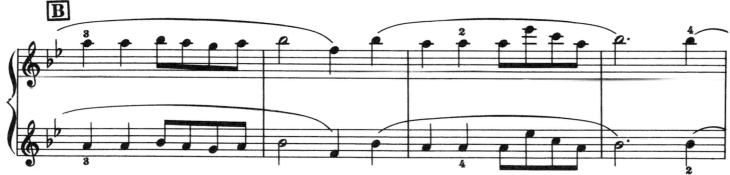

"The Metronome"

Theme from Symphony No. 8

3

Secondo

Ludwig van Beethoven

Lively, mechanical motion

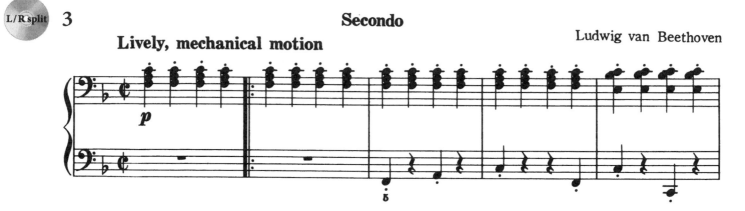

A

poco cresc.   *mf*   *p*

B

poco cresc.   *mf*   *p*   *f*

C

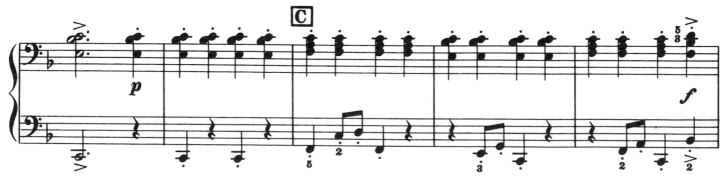

p   *f*

p   1.   2.   *pp*   *sf*

"The Metronome"

Theme from Symphony No. 8

Primo

Lively, mechanical motion

Ludwig van Beethoven

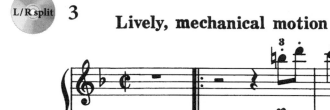

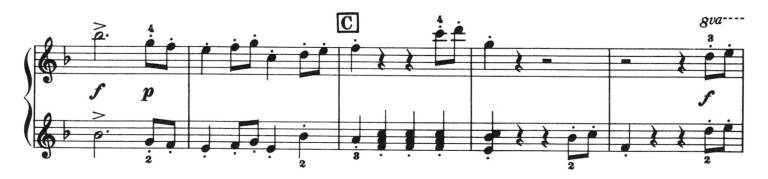

Arioso

Secondo

Johann Sebastian Bach

Moderately slow

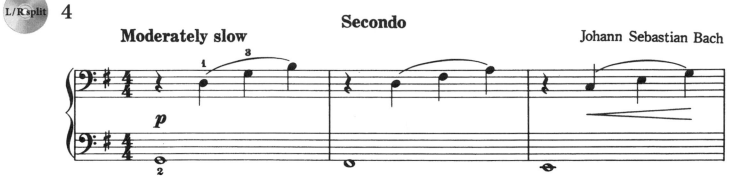

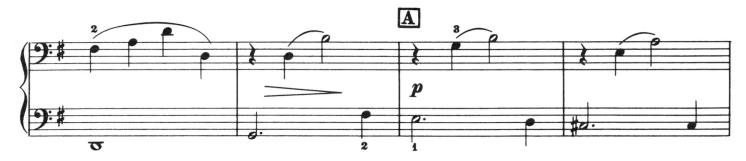

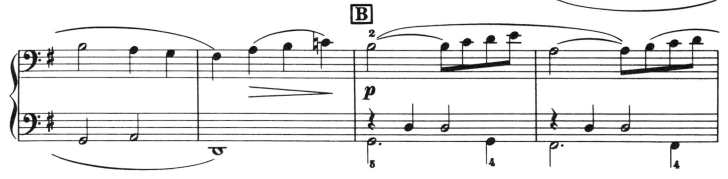

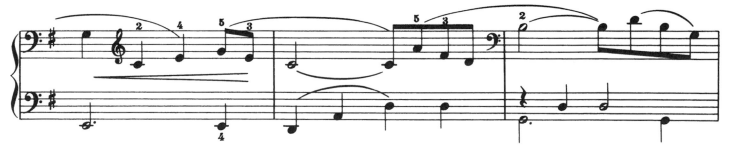

Arioso

Primo

Johann Sebastian Bach

Rondino
Theme from Cello Concerto in D

Secondo

Joseph Haydn

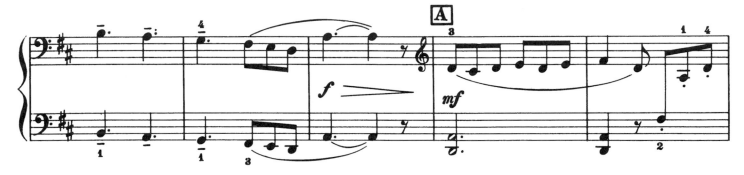

D.C. al Fine

Rondino
Theme from Cello Concerto in D

Primo

Joseph Haydn

D. C. al Fine

Caprice No. 24

Secondo

Niccolo Paganini

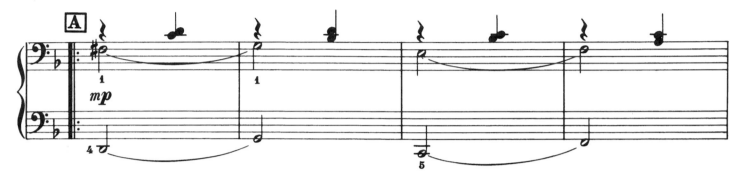

Caprice No. 24

Niccolo Paganini

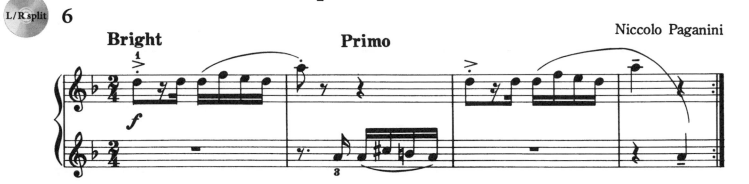

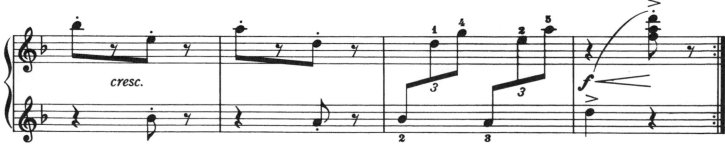

Duet from "Don Giovanni"
("La ci darem la mano")

Wolfgang A. Mozart

Secondo

Duet from "Don Giovanni"

("La ci darem la mano")

Wolfgang A. Mozart

L/R split   7

Melody in Waltz Time

Theme from String Quartet No. 2

Secondo

Alexander Borodin

Moderately; with a lilt

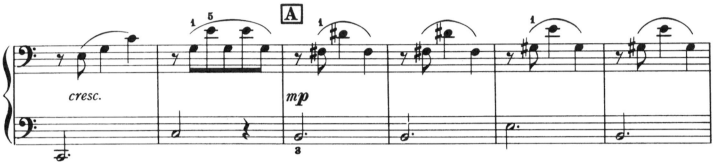

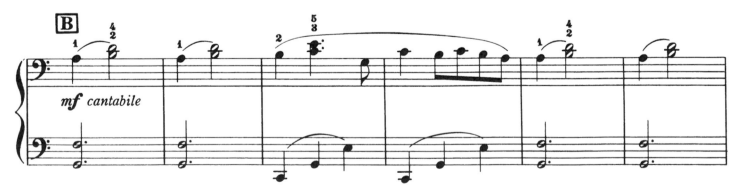

Melody in Waltz Time
Theme from String Quartet No. 2

Primo

Alexander Borodin

Moderately; with a lilt

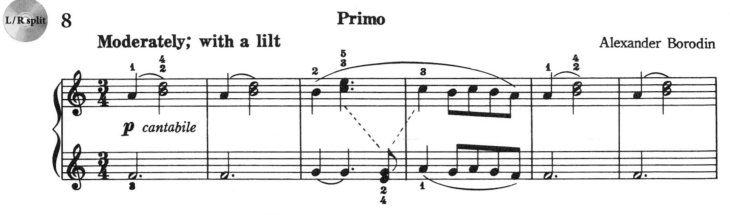

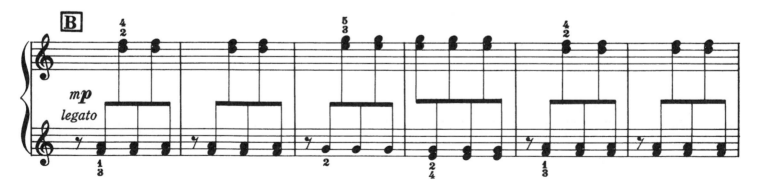

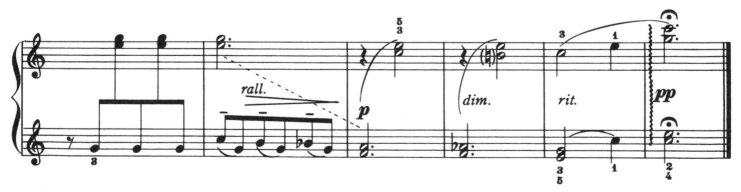

Gavotte from "Classical Symphony"

Secondo

Serge Prokofieff

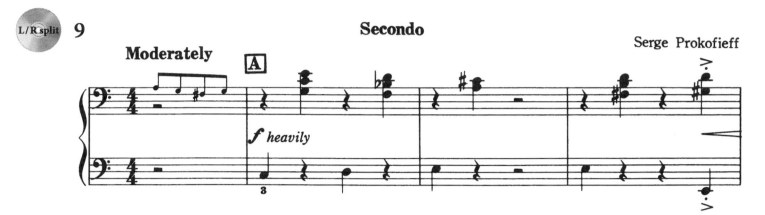

Gavotte from "Classical Symphony"

Primo

Serge Prokofieff

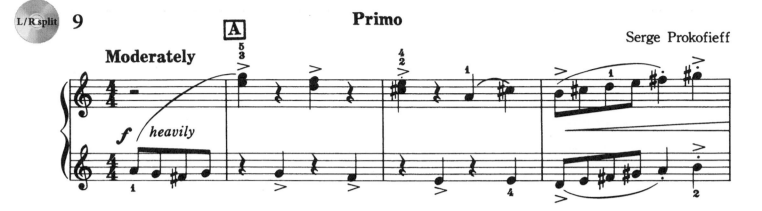

The Musical Snuffbox

Secondo

Anatol Liadov

Lively, mechanical motion

The Musical Snuffbox

Primo

Anatol Liadov

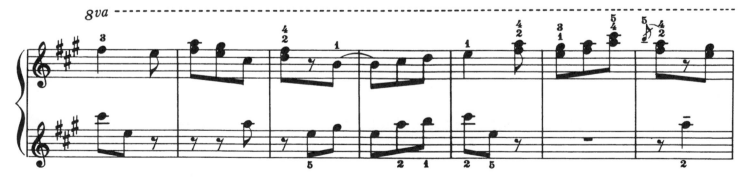

Secondo

The Harmonious Blacksmith
(Theme)

11

Moderately　　　　　　　　　**Secondo**

Georg F. Händel

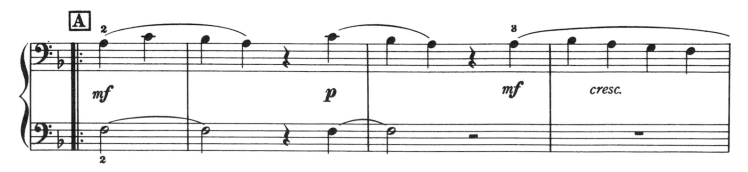

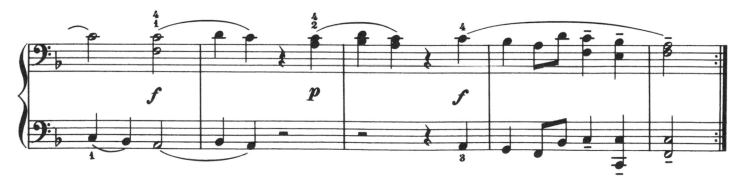

The Harmonious Blacksmith

(Theme)

11

Primo

Georg F. Händel

Moderately

Frolic

Secondo

Béla Bartók

12

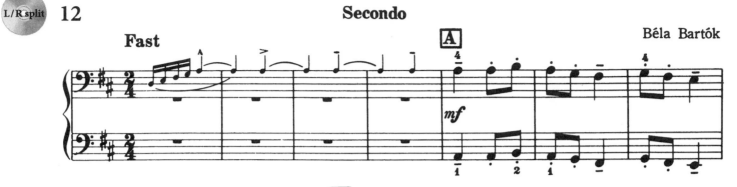

Frolic

Primo

Béla Bartók

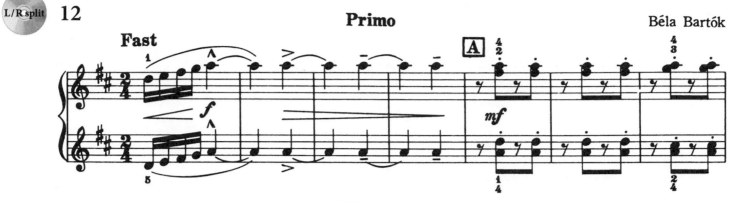

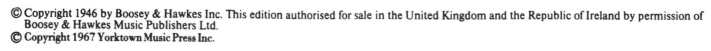

Lullaby from "The Firebird"

Secondo

Igor Stravinsky

Moderately slow

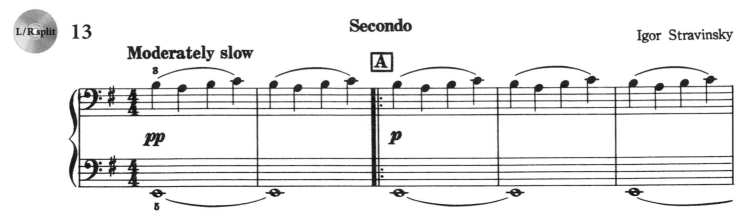

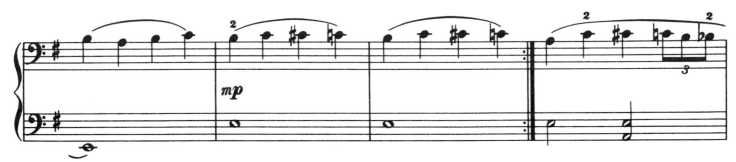

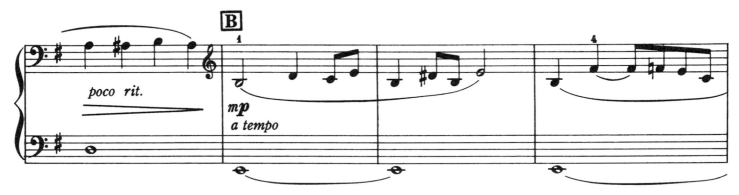

Lullaby from "The Firebird"

Primo

Igor Stravinsky

Trepak
Russian Dance from " The Nutcracker "

14

Very lively

Secondo

Peter I. Tchaikovsky

Trepak
Russian Dance from "The Nutcracker"

L/R split   14

Peter I. Tchaikovsky

Very lively   **Primo**

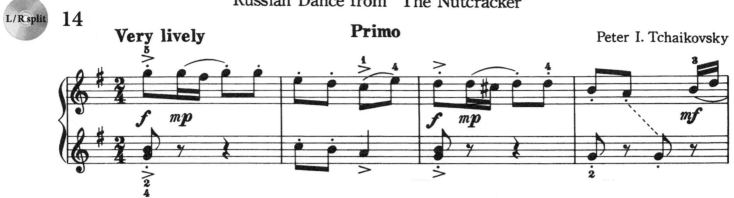

Minuet
from "A Little Night Music"

Secondo

Wolfgang A. Mozart

Minuet
from "A Little Night Music"

Primo

Wolfgang A. Mozart

Secondo

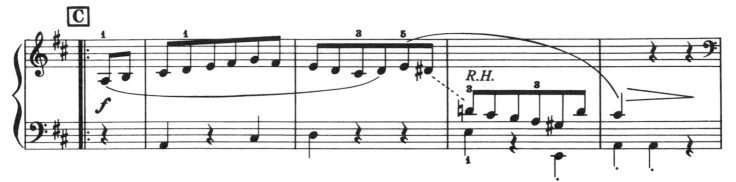

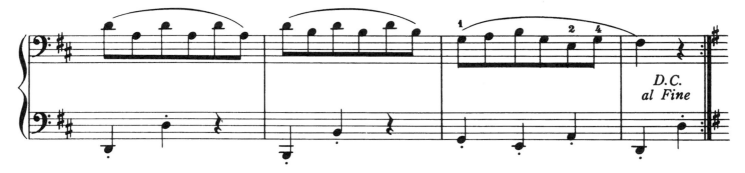

The Streets of Laredo

Secondo

Cowboy Song

The Streets of Laredo

16 Cowboy Song

Primo

Moderately

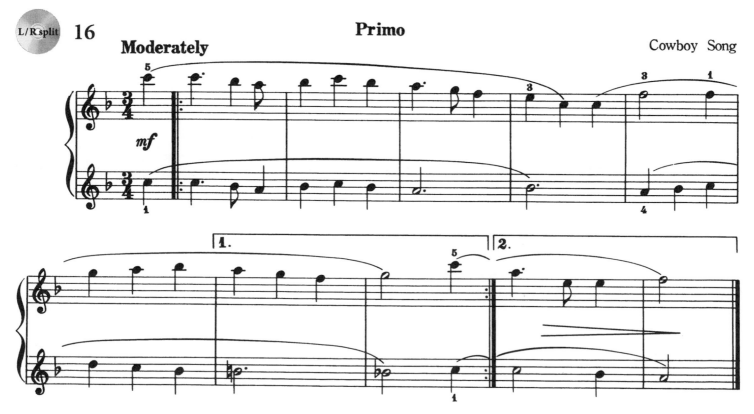

The Comedians' Galop

Secondo

Dmitri Kabalevsky

Very bright; with humor

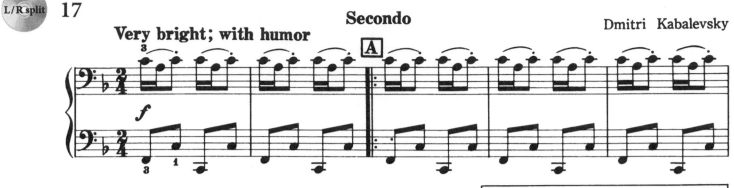

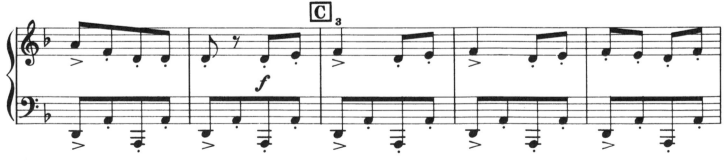

The Comedians' Galop

17

Primo

Dmitri Kabalevsky

Very bright; with humor

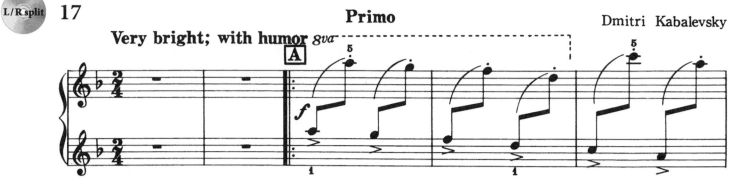

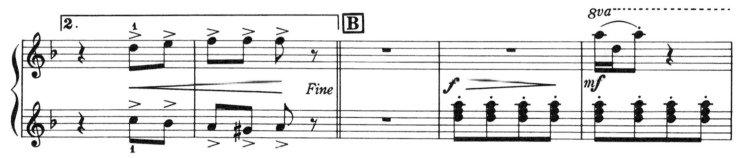

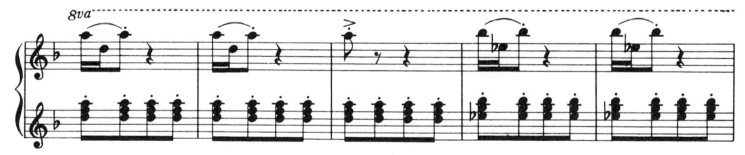

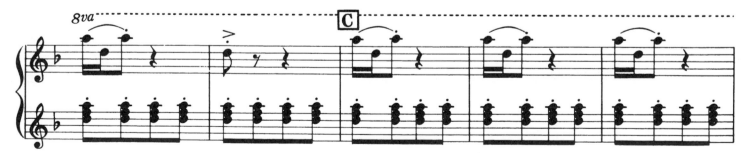

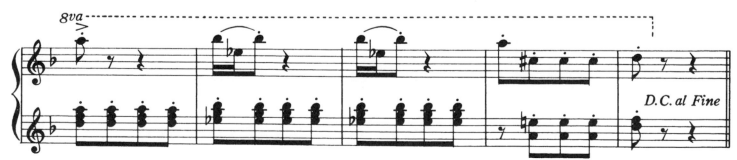

Little Rhapsody
on Hungarian themes

Denes Agay

Secondo

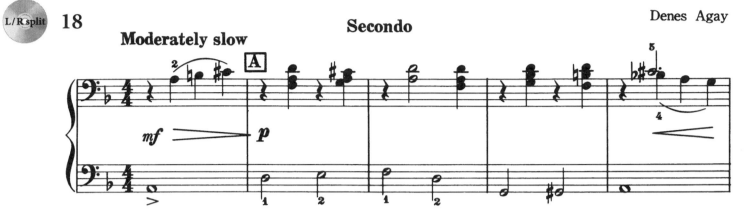

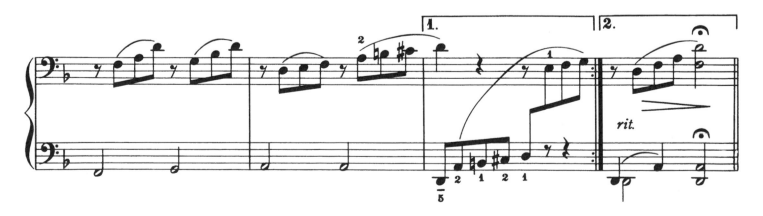

Little Rhapsody

on Hungarian themes

Primo

Denes Agay

L/R split 18

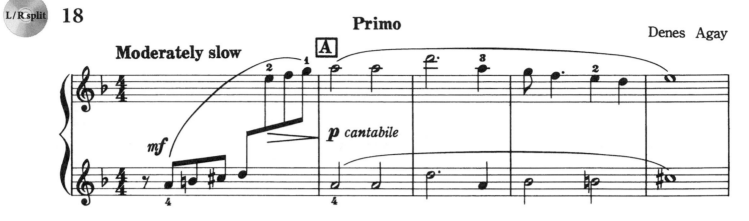

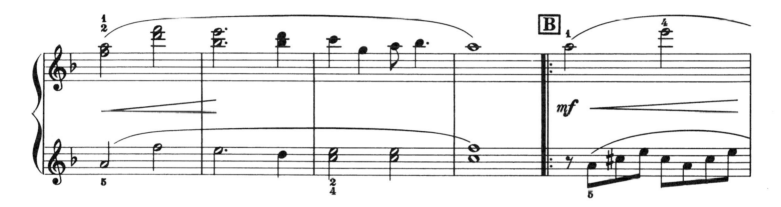

Secondo

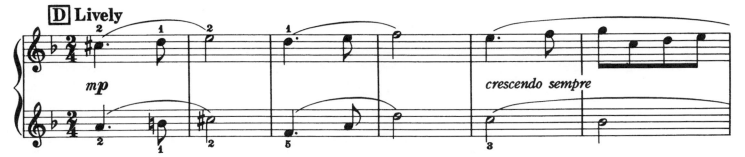

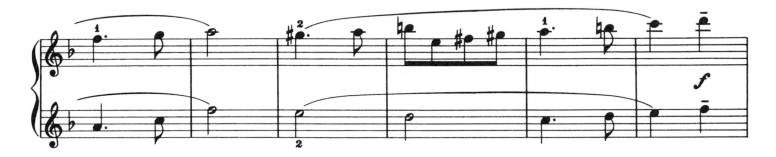

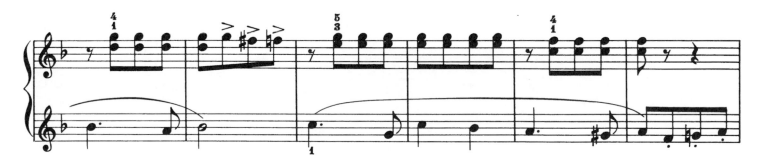

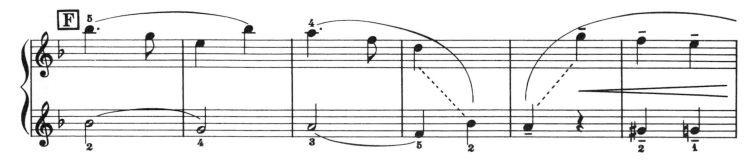

The "Merry Boys" Polka

19

Secondo

Franz von Suppé

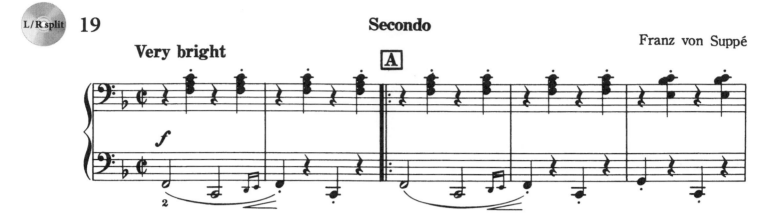

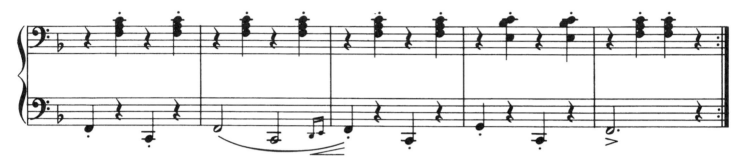

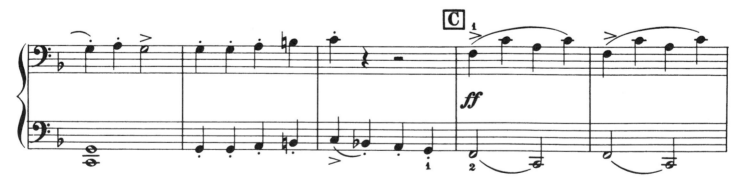

The "Merry Boys" Polka

19 **Primo**

Franz von Suppé

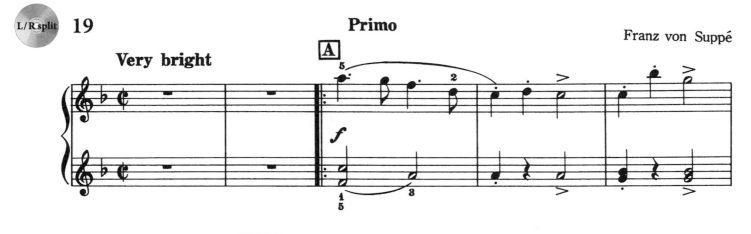

2 cross over right hand

Waltzes
from "Fledermaus" and "Gypsy Baron"

20

Secondo

Johann Strauss

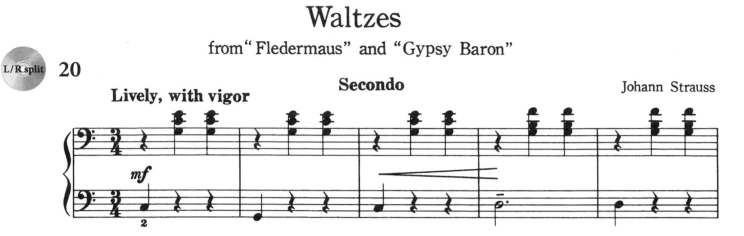

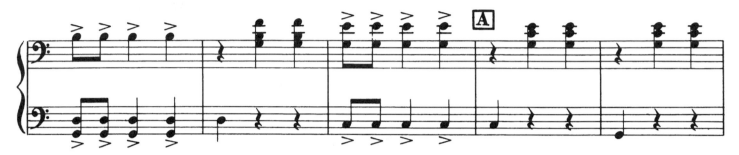

Waltzes
from " Fledermaus" and "Gypsy Baron"

20

Primo

Johann Strauss

Lively, with vigor

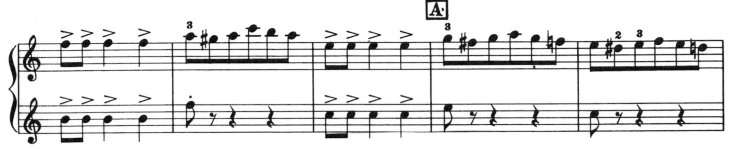

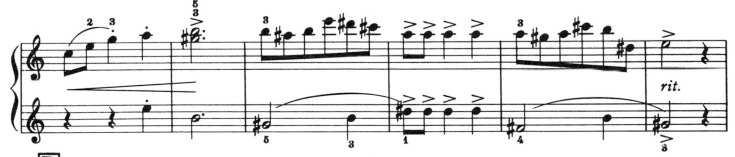

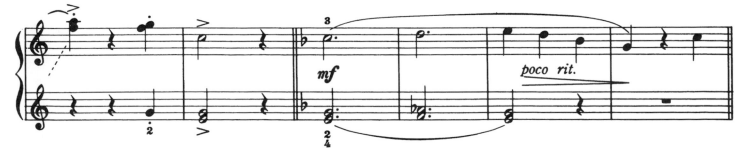

Secondo

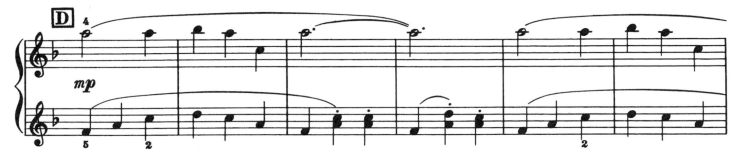

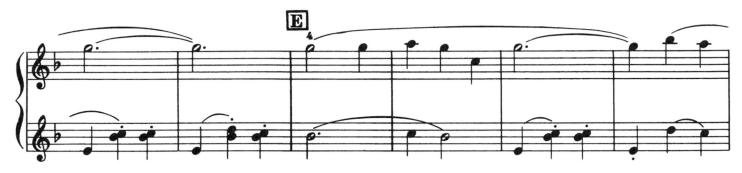

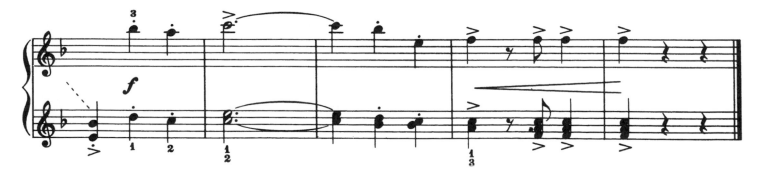

The Washington Post

Secondo

John Philip Sousa

Lively march tempo

The Washington Post

Primo

John Philip Sousa

21

Lively march tempo

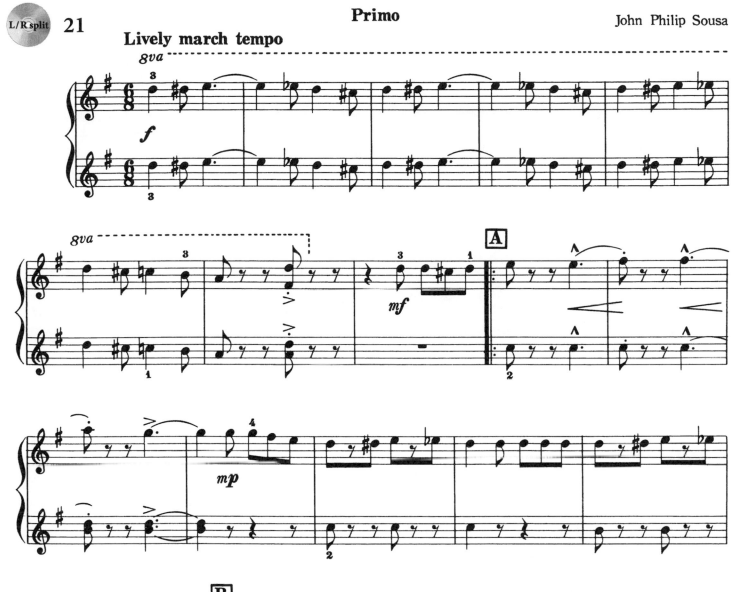

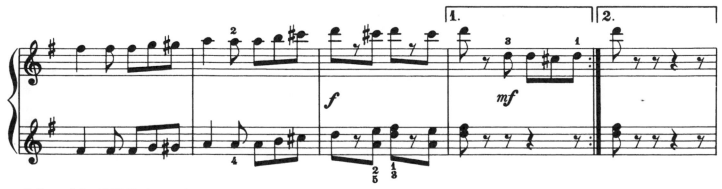

Secondo

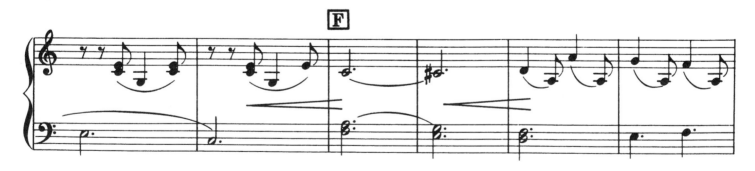

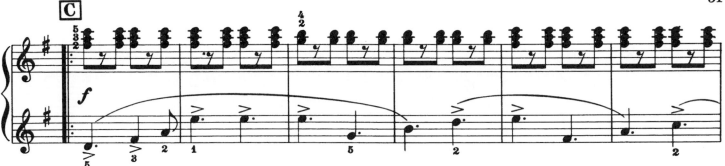

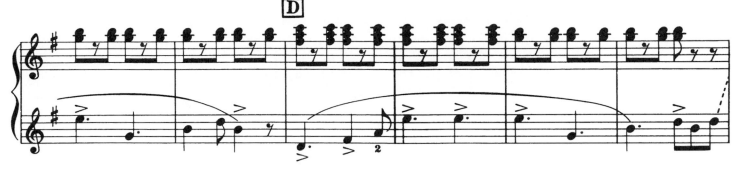

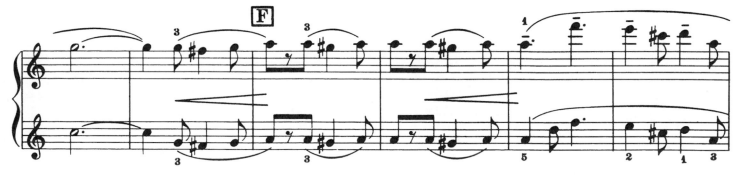

Fascination

L/R split 22

Secondo

Filippo D. Marchetti

Slow waltz

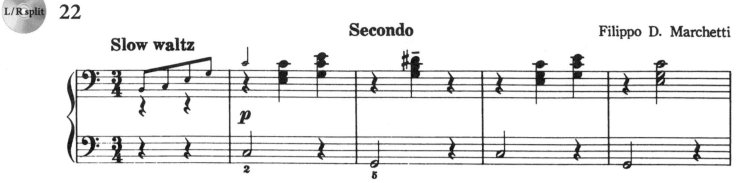

Fascination

Primo

Filippo D. Marchetti

L/R split 22

Slow waltz

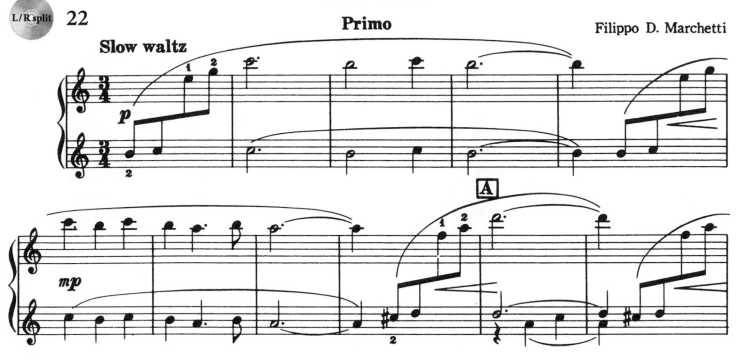

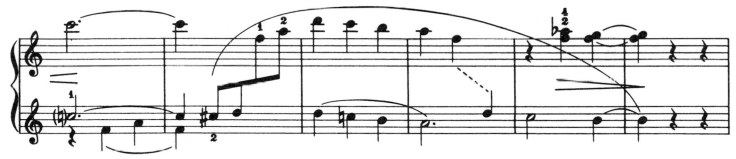

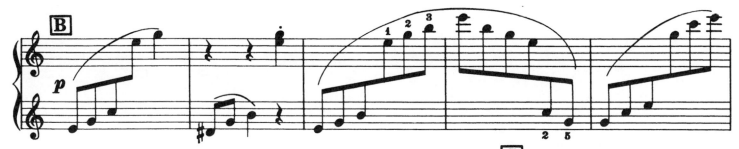

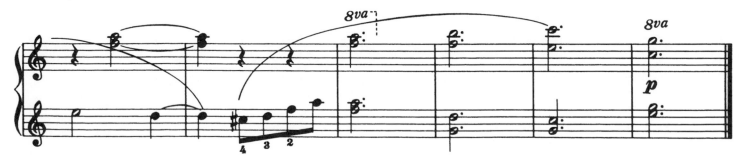

Can - Can
from the Operetta "La Vie Parisienne"

23

Jacques Offenbach

Secondo

Can - Can
from the Operetta "La Vie Parisienne"

Jacques Offenbach

Primo

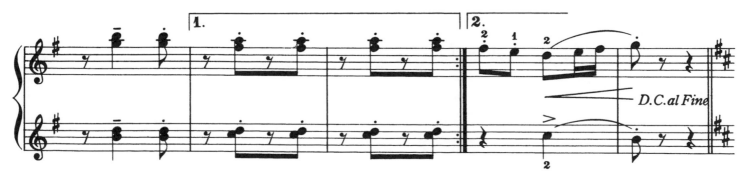

Parade Of The Tin Soldiers

Secondo

24

Leon Jessel

Graceful marching tempo

Parade Of The Tin Soldiers

Primo

Leon Jessel

Graceful marching tempo

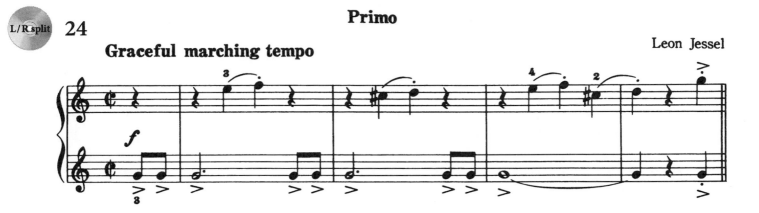

Secondo

The Banjo Rag

Secondo

Charles Drumheller

25

The Banjo Rag

Primo

Charles Drumheller

25

Lively

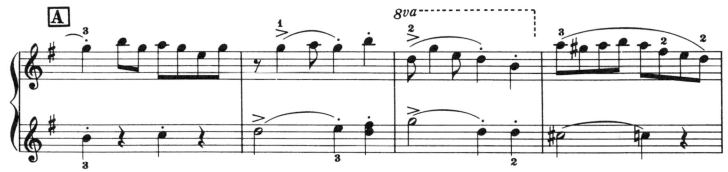

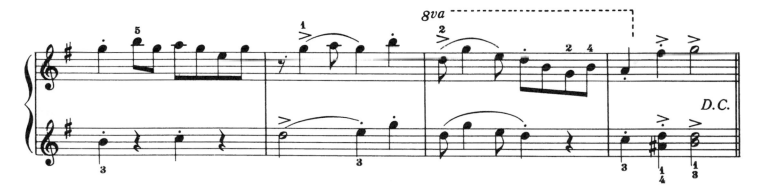

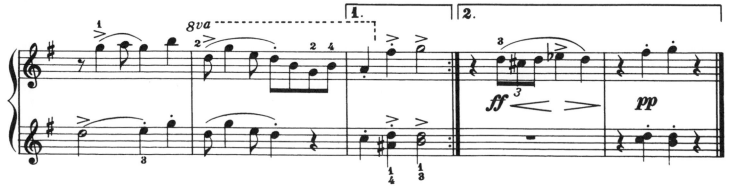

Careless Love

Secondo

Folk Song

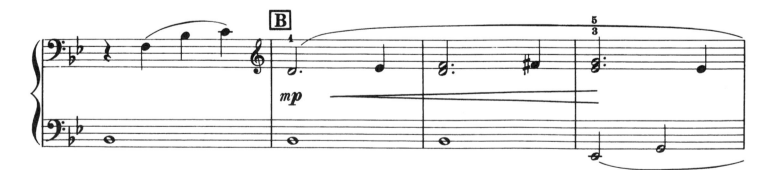

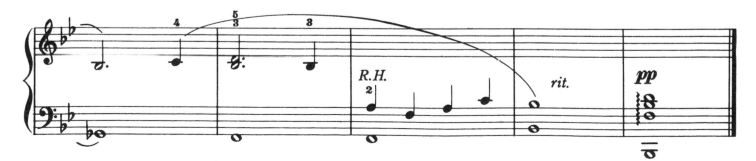

Careless Love

26

Primo

Folk Song

Arkansas Traveler

Secondo

Fiddle Tune

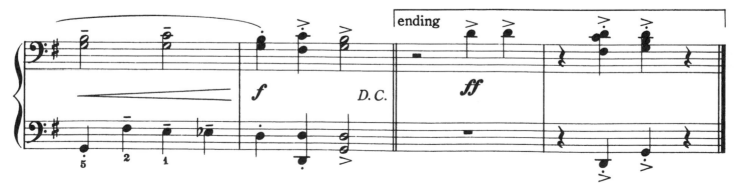

Arkansas Traveler

Primo

Fiddle Tune

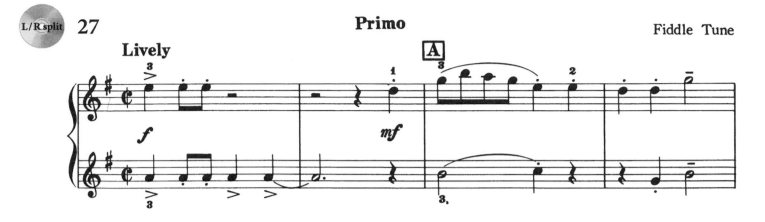

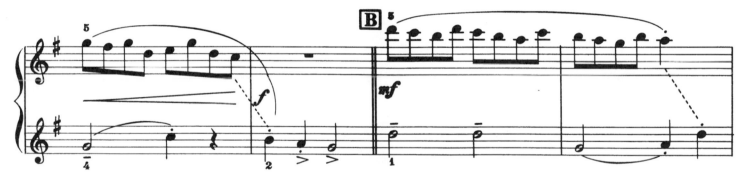

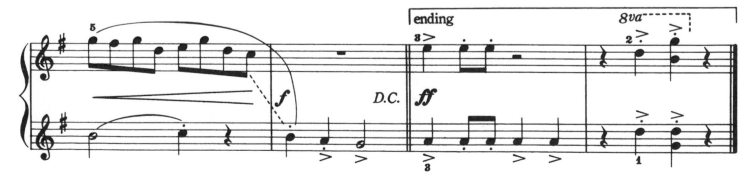

Hush - A - Bye

(All The Pretty Little Horses)

Secondo

Folk Lullaby

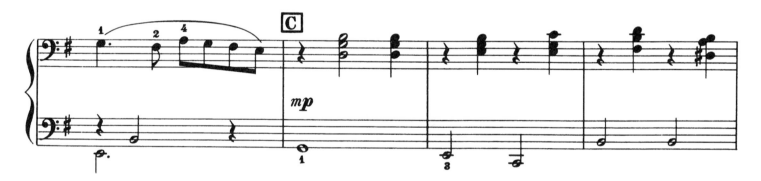

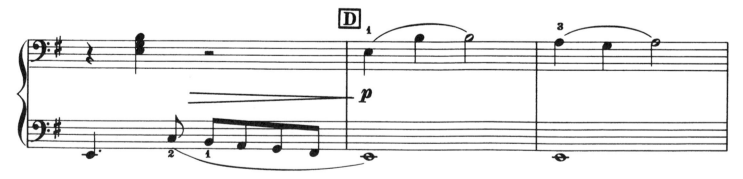

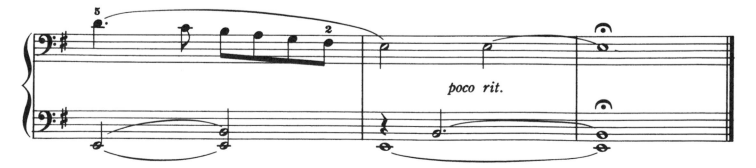

Hush-A-Bye
(All The Pretty Little Horses)

Primo

Folk Lullaby

28

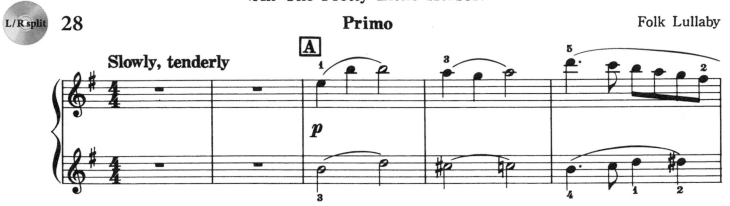

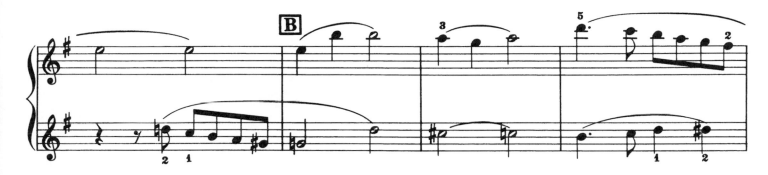

Adios Muchachos

Secondo

Julio Sanders

Moderate tango tempo

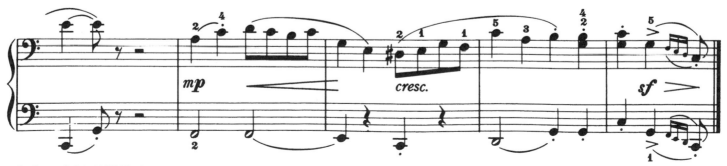

Adios Muchachos

29

Moderate tango tempo   **Primo**

Julio Sanders

Boogie For Two

Secondo

Bright; with a rhythmic drive

Gerald Martin

Boogie For Two

Primo

Gerald Martin

Secondo

Primo

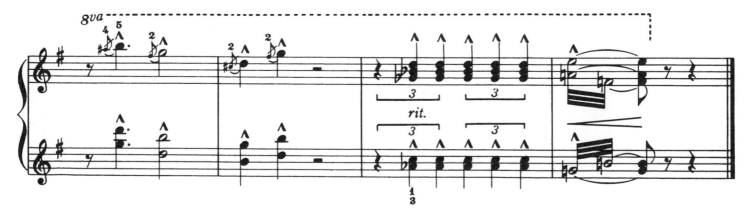

Give My Regards To Broadway

31 L/R split

Secondo

George M. Cohan

Brightly

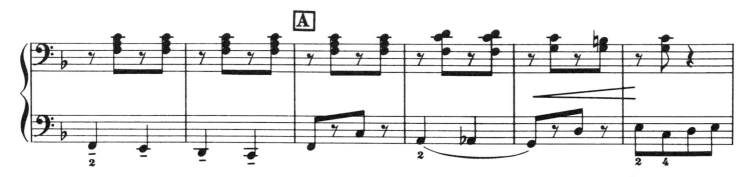

Give My Regards To Broadway

Primo

George M. Cohan

Jamaica Farewell

Secondo

Calypso Song

32

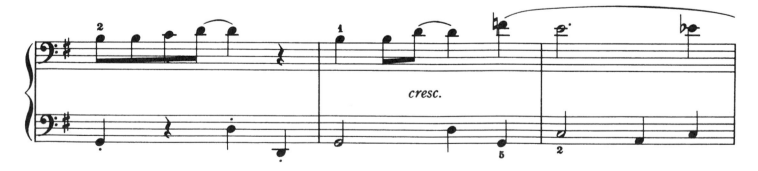

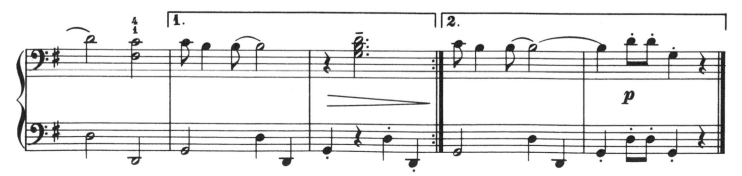

Jamaica Farewell

Primo

Calypso Song

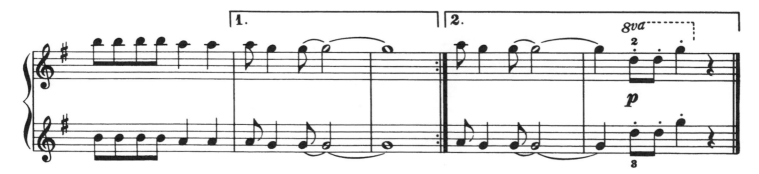

O Come All Ye Faithful

Adeste Fideles

Secondo

Old Latin Hymn

Spirited walking tempo

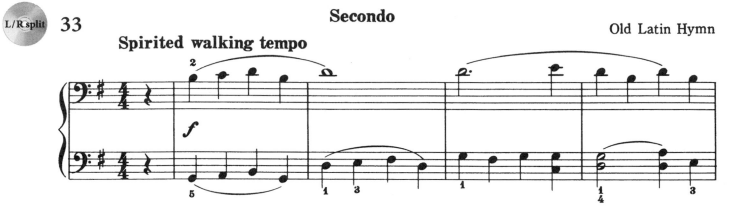

O Come All Ye Faithful

Adeste Fideles

Primo

Old Latin Hymn

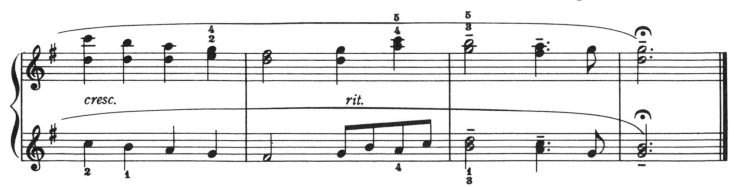